Twelve Short Stories for Le

EASY READING
for ESL Students

BOOK 3

by Johnny Bread

CANADIAN LANGUAGE SCHOOL

INTRODUCTION

Easy Reading for ESL Students – Book 3 is a comprehensive reader designed especially for intermediate and advanced students of English as a Second Language. The book was developed and tested by full-time teachers of English.

There are twelve short stories. Each story is designed to engage students in a well-rounded language learning experience. There are comprehension, vocabulary, speaking and writing exercises after each story.

The stories are entertaining and have plot twists and surprise endings. Teachers of English as a Second Language will enjoy using them to engage students on a wide range of topics and interests.

The stories are short (400 – 500 words). Each story and its exercises can be completed in 60 minutes.

You can download a free audio version of the book read by a professional actor. See page 76.

CONTENTS

Jumbo   4

El Doctor   10

The Tagger   16

The Puzzle   22

Hungry as a St. Bernard   28

My Friend Burglar   34

The Coach   40

The Jester   46

A Miracle   52

Buddy   58

The Kickboxer   64

The Runner   70

JUMBO

Mani had a little hardware store in town. He worked very hard, but business was not very good. Mani hoped that his luck would change, and one day it did.

Every Friday, after Mani closed the store, he went to a restaurant to meet with other store owners. He had many friends among them. They mostly talked about business, but they talked about other things too.

One day Mani disappeared. For three months nobody saw him. Then one day he showed up at the restaurant. He looked very happy.

"Where have you been, Mani?" his friends asked. "And why do you look so happy?"

"I look happy, because I am happy," Mani said. "I have inherited something big – something really big from my uncle."

"What have you inherited?" one of his friends asked.

"An elephant," Mani said happily.

"An elephant? You're joking!" his friend shouted in surprise. All the people in the restaurant were listening now.

"No, I am not. His name is Jumbo. He is the best thing that has ever happened to me."

"You're joking," his friend repeated.

"No, I am not," Mani said again. "Jumbo has brought joy to my family. He lives in my garden. My children ride him and play with him every day. My wife has flowers in the garden. Jumbo takes care of them. When he sees a weed, he pulls it out. When the flowers need water, he goes to the pool, fills his trunk with water and waters them. And he guards my house. Nobody dares approach my house when we are not home."

A rich store owner came up to Mani and said, "I want to buy Jumbo. My life hasn't been very happy lately."

"Jumbo is not for sale," Mani said.

"I'll give you $20,000."

"Jumbo is a member of my family. I really can't."

"$200,000," the man said.

"You know," Mani said. "Sometimes when I feel a little sad, Jumbo comes up to me and puts his trunk around me. He's a real friend. You don't sell your friends, do you?"

"$2,000,000," the man said.

"OK," Mani said.

So the man bought Jumbo for $2,000,000 and took him home. Nobody saw the man for three months.

Then one day he showed up in the restaurant. He looked miserable.

"What happened to you?" Mani asked.

"I am the unhappiest man in the world," the man said. "It's Jumbo, the elephant. My children are scared of him. He destroyed my wife's flowers. His droppings are everywhere. He is so noisy that all my neighbors hate me. He got angry with me once, and he hit me with his trunk and kicked me. I am so miserable."

"Shh," Mani said. "Not so loud, or you will never sell him."

Notes

_____

_____

_____

I. Choose the right answer.

1. Mani owned a _____.
    a. grocery store
    b. computer store
    c. hardware store

2. Mani's business was _____.
    a. very successful
    b. not very successful
    c. OK

3. Every Friday Mani went _____.
    a. on a trip
    b. to a concert
    c. to a restaurant

4. Mani inherited _____.
    a. an elephant
    b. ten million dollars
    c. a hardware store

5. Mani sold Jumbo for _____.
    a. $2,000,000
    b. $200,000
    c. $20,000

6. Mani was _____.
    a. an honest man
    b. a liar
    c. a good merchant

II. **Complete the sentences with the words from the box below.**

weed	trunk	~~hardware~~	dry
dares	droppings	destroyed	inherited

1. Mani sold tools for workshops and gardens in his store. It was a little _hardware_ store.

2. When Mani's uncle died, he left an elephant to Mani. Mani _____ an elephant.

3. A wild plant growing where it is not wanted is called a _____.

4. When the flowers were _____, Jumbo watered them.

5. Jumbo used his _____ to water the flowers.

6. Mani said, "Jumbo is a good guard. Nobody _____ approach the house."

7. Jumbo did a lot of damage to Mani's garden. He _____ it.

8. The garden was Jumbo's bathroom. His _____ were everywhere.

III. **Choose two words from the box on the previous page and write a short paragraph using them.**

_____
_____
_____
_____

IV. **Complete the sentences with the expressions from the box below.**

| got angry | luck would change |
| brought joy | looked miserable |

1. Mani hoped for a better life. He hoped his _____.

2. Mani's family loved Jumbo very much. He _____ to their lives.

3. The man was very unhappy. He _____.

4. Jumbo _____ with the man, and he kicked him.

V. **Choose two expressions from the box above and write a short paragraph using them.**

_____
_____
_____
_____

VI. Answer the question in full sentences.

1. What did Mani do for a living?
2. How was business at his store?
3. What did Mani hope for?
4. Where did he go every Friday?
5. Why did he go there?
6. What happened one day?
7. What did Mani say to his friends?
8. Why did the rich store owner want to buy Jumbo?
9. Why did Mani lie about Jumbo?

VII. Oral Summary

Retell the story in a few sentences.

VIII. Written Summary

Write a few sentences to summarize the story.

_____
_____
_____
_____
_____
_____
_____
_____

EL DOCTOR

His real name was John Ayala, but everybody in America called him *El Doctor*. He was a doctor and an adventurer rolled into one.

John became a doctor because he thought it might open doors to the most forbidden places – and he was right.

He studied at Harvard Medical School, and worked at the best hospital in the country. Then one day adventure called out, and he was gone.

He went to the Amazon, and he lived with different Indian tribes for many years. Since he was a doctor, and he was helping people, the Indians usually accepted him. He lived in many unimaginable places in South America. He stayed with the Indians for a while, and then he moved on. *El Doctor*, as they called him, became famous and well-respected.

When John finally returned home and settled in Boston, he was often invited to parties. People liked his stories. When he started to speak, everybody was quiet and listened. One day some people asked him to tell a story. He smiled and began to speak.

"One day I heard about a tribe that lived deep in the rainforest. People said the tribe lived the same kind of life as their ancestors did hundreds of years ago. Progress had stopped. The tribe was wild and also a little dangerous. Nobody dared approach the tribe.

I didn't need to hear any more. I went to look for them. But this time, I was not so lucky.

When I finally met them in the rainforest, they weren't friendly to me at all.

I am *El Doctor*, and I have come to help you, I said. Have you heard about *El Doctor*? They obviously had not because, without a word, they tied me up and pulled me into their village. I was a prisoner. For the first time in my life I was afraid. I thought I was going to die.

Pure chance saved me. The chief's daughter got very ill, and everybody thought she was going to die. They didn't understand the word doctor, so I told them I was a shaman in my country and could help the girl. They brought me to the chief. Surprisingly, he agreed to let me examine his daughter. I instantly knew what was wrong with her. She needed her appendix removed and very quickly. I removed it, and three days later the girl was healthy again.

That day I became their shaman, and everybody started to respect me. I stayed with them, helping them with their little health problems. The girl I had saved, was very curious and very clever. She often helped me treat my patients."

"What was the girl's name and what became of her?" a woman asked.

"Her name is Anaea," John said with a smile. "She became a doctor and works here in Boston. She is also my wife and is sitting next to me."

Everybody looked at a dark woman sitting next to John. She was wearing a beautiful smile.

Notes

I. Choose the right answer.

1. John Ayala was a doctor and _____.
    a. a lawyer
    b. an athlete
    c. an adventurer

2. John went to live in _____.
    a. South Africa
    b. South America
    c. South Europe

3. John lived with _____.
    a. Brazilian soccer players
    b. Argentinian gauchos
    c. Indian tribes

4. When John met the tribe, they _____.
    a. tied him up
    b. feared him and ran away
    c. welcomed him

5. John stayed alive because _____.
    a. he saved the chief's daughter's life
    b. he called the American Embassy
    c. he escaped

6. John _____ the chief's daughter.
    a. adopted
    b. married
    c. didn't like

II. **Complete the sentences with the words from the box below.**

unimaginable	instantly	~~forbidden~~	tied
surprisingly	moved on	obviously	removed

1. There are places where people can't go. Sometimes we call them _forbidden_ places.

2. John lived in strange places. He lived in _____ places.

3. John never stayed long in one place. He stayed for a while, and then he _____.

4. John tried to explain to the Indians who he was, but _____ they didn't understand.

5. The Indians _____ John up. He was a prisoner.

6. John didn't expect the chief to let him examine his daughter, but _____ he agreed.

7. John was a doctor. He _____ knew what was wrong with the chief's daughter.

8. John _____ the girl's appendix, and three days later she was healthy again.

III. **Choose two words from the box on the previous page and write a short paragraph using them.**

_____
_____
_____
_____

IV. **Complete the sentences with the expressions from the box below.**

| pure chance | became of |
| adventure called out | rolled into one |

1. John was a doctor and an adventurer _____.

2. One day John was gone because _____ to him.

3. The chief's daughter got sick, and it saved John's life. It was _____.

4. The woman wanted to know what the girl was doing today – what _____ her.

V. **Choose two expressions from the box above and write a short paragraph using these expressions.**

_____
_____
_____
_____

VI. Answer the questions in full sentences.

1. Who was John Ayala?
2. Why did he become a doctor?
3. Where did he go when adventure called out to him?
4. What did he do there?
5. Why was he accepted by Indian tribes?
6. What happened to him one day?
7. What saved his life?
8. How did it change his situation in the tribe?
9. Who did he marry?

VII. Oral Summary

Retell the story in a few sentences.

VIII. Written Summary

Write a few sentences to summarize the story.

_____
_____
_____
_____
_____
_____
_____
_____

THE TAGGER

Two little boys were playing near the water. Their names were Christopher and Paul. They were four years old. They were playing with a little sailboat, and they were fighting. It was Christopher's sailboat, and he didn't want to let Paul play with it. Nobody was watching the boys.

Suddenly two police cars arrived. A policeman got out of each car. One of them grabbed Christopher, and the other grabbed Paul. The policemen dragged the boys to their cars. Paul started to cry.

"Wait!" Christopher shouted. "Let me give this to my brother. I don't want him to cry." The policeman let Christopher go, and he gave his sailboat to Paul. Then the policemen put the boys into their cars and drove away. The boys were scared to death and had no idea where the policemen were taking them.

Twenty-five years later a police car was cruising down the street. It was around midnight, and it was dark outside. Two policemen were in the car. The policeman at the wheel was Paul Henderson.

Paul noticed a man standing on the sidewalk. He stopped the car and watched him. The man was painting on the building.

"A tagger," Paul said to his partner with contempt. "Damn taggers are ruining this town. I hate them so much. I have been trying to stop them for quite some time. They belong in prison, all of them."

Paul was looking at the picture on the wall. Suddenly he got interested in what the man was painting. The picture didn't look bad at all. It was a sailboat on a lake. It reminded him of something, but he couldn't remember what it was.

Paul got out of the car and walked to the tagger. He grabbed his shoulder and turned him around. Paul was staring at the man's face in amazement. The face that was staring back was his own.

At the police station Paul checked the man's ID. *Christopher Henderson, born on March 12.* The man had the same name and the same birthday as he did, and he looked exactly like him. This man was his twin brother! There was no question about it.

Christopher went to prison for damaging several buildings.

"We grew up in two different foster families because our parents couldn't take care of us," Paul said to his friends. "I didn't know about him. I became a policeman, and he became a criminal. Isn't that amazing?"

A year later Christopher was released from prison. Paul was waiting for him outside.

"Hi bro," Paul said. I remember now what you gave me twenty-six years ago. Today, you will get it back."

They drove together to the lake. When they got there, Christopher couldn't believe his eyes. There on the lake was a sailboat. But it was not a toy – it was a real one.

Notes

_____

_____

_____

_____

I. Choose the right answer.

1. The little sailboat belonged to _____.
    a. Christopher
    b. Paul
    c. a policeman

2. The policemen took the boys _____.
    a. to an amusement park
    b. to the police station
    c. to an unknown place

3. Paul became a _____.
    a. tagger
    b. driver
    c. policeman

4. Paul hated _____.
    a. policemen
    b. taggers
    c. his brother

5. Christopher became a _____.
    a. policeman
    b. criminal
    c. famous painter

6. Paul gave Christopher a _____.
    a. sailboat
    b. car
    c. paintbrush

II. **Complete the sentences with the words from the box below.**

cruising	sailboat	contempt	foster
staring	dragged	~~graffiti~~	grabbed

1. Drawings on buildings are often called _graffiti_____.

2. A boat propelled by wind is called a _____.

3. The policemen _____ the boys to their cars because the boys didn't want to go.

4. The police car was going very slowly. The driver was _____ down the street.

5. Paul hated taggers and didn't respect them. He spoke about them with _____.

6. Paul put his hand on the man's shoulder and held him tight. He _____ him.

7. Paul was looking at the man's face in surprise. He was _____ at him.

8. A family that takes care of a child that isn't their own is called a _____ family.

III. **Choose two words from the box on the previous page and write a short paragraph using them.**

_____
_____
_____
_____

IV. **Complete the sentences with the expressions from the box below.**

| no question about it | scared to death |
| at the wheel | staring back |

1. The boys were frightened. They were _____.

2. Paul was driving the police car. He was _____.

3. The man was looking at Paul in amazement too. He was _____.

4. There was no doubt the man was Paul's twin brother. There was _____.

V. **Choose two expressions from the box above and write a short paragraph using these expressions.**

_____
_____
_____
_____

VI. Answer the questions in full sentences.

1. What were the boys' names?
2. How old were they at the beginning of the story?
3. What were they doing when the police arrived?
4. What did the police do?
5. What did Christopher give Paul?
6. Which of the two boys become a policeman?
7. What happened one night twenty-five years later?
8. Who was the tagger?
9. What did Paul give Christopher?

VII. Summary

Retell the story in a few sentences.

VIII. Written Summary

Write a few sentences to summarize the story.

_____
_____
_____
_____
_____
_____
_____
_____

THE PUZZLE

A rider was slowly riding his horse through a dark forest. He was lost and was riding in circles. The rider was wearing fine clothes like noblemen do, but he was not a man. He was a boy. What was a little boy doing in the forest in the middle of the night?

Suddenly he stopped and peered through the darkness. There was an old woman walking just a few feet away from him.

"Wait!" he shouted at the old woman. "You have to tell me the way to the castle."

The woman didn't stop and kept walking.

"Stop at once!" the boy shouted again. "Do you not know who I am? I am the prince, the future king."

The woman stopped and turned around. "To me you are a spoiled brat. I haven't heard you say the magic word *please*," she said. Then she continued walking.

"Please," the boy said. "I need your help. I got lost during the hunt, and I've been riding in circles for hours. I'm tired."

The woman stopped again. "Follow me," she said. "You will sleep at my house. Tomorrow I will show you the way."

The boy's name was Henry, and he really was the future king. The woman's name was Clara, and she was a medicine woman living alone in the forest. The year was 1502.

Henry and Clara spent only a few hours together, but they started to like each other.

The next morning when Henry was leaving, he said, "Thank you very much for everything. May I come visit you from time to time?"

"You may come whenever you want," Clara said. "Take care of yourself, Henry."

From that time on Henry often visited Clara. She became his new grandmother. She was very clever, and whenever Henry needed advice she was there for him.

The years went by. Henry grew up. When he was twenty years old, the king, his father, called him and told him, "It's time for you to get married, my son. I have invited twenty of the finest princesses from around the world. You will choose one of them."

Henry ran to the forest to find Clara. "You've got to help me, Clara. I don't want to get married, at least not now."

Clara smiled. "Tell them you will marry the one who can solve Clara's puzzle.

"What puzzle, grandma?"

"I had five apples in a basket. Five dwarfs came to my house, and I gave each dwarf one apple. The dwarfs left. One apple remained in the basket. How did I do it?"

The twenty princesses arrived at the castle. Nineteen of them had no idea how to solve the puzzle. They even got angry. They thought he was making fun of them. Then one of them, called Isabel, smiled and said, "I think you want to marry me. Otherwise the puzzle would be more difficult than that. The last dwarf walked away with the basket."

Was Isabel right? Did Henry marry her?

Notes

I. Choose the right answer.

1. The rider was _____.
    a. the king
    b. a boy
    c. a medicine man

2. The rider saw _____ walking by.
    a. an old woman
    b. an old man
    c. a deer

3. The old woman was _____.
    a. Henry's mother
    b. a magician
    c. a medicine woman

4. At first Henry was _____.
    a. polite
    b. rude
    c. happy

5. Henry didn't want to _____.
    a. stay single
    b. be a king
    c. get married

6. _____ solved the puzzle.
    a. Isabel
    b. Nobody
    c. Everybody

II. **Complete the sentences with the words from the box below.**

| really | fine | magic | remained |
| fun | darkness | brat | ~~circles~~ |

1. A rider rode for some time and then returned to the same place. He rode in _circles_____.

2. The rider was wearing nice, expensive clothes. He was wearing _____ clothes.

3. He couldn't see very well through the _____.

4. A child who makes trouble all the time is sometimes called a spoiled _____.

5. A thing that has special powers is _____.

6. What Henry told Clara was the truth. He _____ was the future king.

7. There were five apples in the basket. Then there was just one. One _____ in the basket.

8. The princesses got angry. They thought that he was making _____ of them.

III. Choose two words from the box on the previous page and write a short paragraph using them.

_____
_____
_____
_____

IV. Complete the sentences with the expressions from the box below.

solve the puzzle	medicine woman
show you the way	whenever you want

1. Clara wanted to lead Henry to the castle. She said, "I'll _____."

2. Clara used herbs from the forest to help people. She was a _____.

3. Clara told Henry he could come any time. She said, "Come _____."

4. Isabel found the solution. She knew how to _____.

V. Choose two expressions from the box above and write a short paragraph using them.

_____
_____
_____
_____

VI. Answer the questions in full sentences.

1. What was the rider like?
2. Who was he?
3. Why was he in the forest in the middle of the night?
4. Who did he see in the forest?
5. Why was the old woman upset with him?
6. How did she help him that night?
7. What did the king tell Henry when he was twenty?
8. How did Clara try to help him?
9. What happened in the end?

VII. Oral Summary

Retell the story in a few sentences.

VIII. Written Summary

Write a few sentences to summarize the story.

_____
_____
_____
_____
_____
_____
_____
_____

HUNGRY AS A ST. BERNARD

Archie Trump was in trouble, and he knew it. After trying to find the way back to his cottage for five hours, he finally admitted to himself that he had gotten lost.

Archie had gone on a hike in the mountains with Steven, Sarah and Jude. They had been hiking for two hours when the weather suddenly changed. It started to snow heavily, and it got very windy. His friends decided to return to the cottage. Archie didn't want to return, and he continued on alone. Now he knew he had made a mistake. He was angry with himself for being so stubborn.

Archie got down on his knees. He couldn't continue anymore. He was exhausted. "Am I going to die?" he asked himself.

Suddenly Archie noticed that something was moving in front of him. He couldn't see it very well because of the falling snow, but he knew what it was. "A bear," he whispered. "Oh my God!"

Archie knew what to do. He had to play dead. He had read that somewhere. He lay down, closed his eyes and waited.

The bear got close and started to sniff him. Archie held his breath and didn't move. He was waiting for the end, but it never came.

When the bear started to lick his face, Archie opened his eyes. It was not a bear. It was a dog – a St. Bernard. The dog was trying to make Archie follow him.

Archie was very lucky after all. The dog led him to a small mountain hotel. It was just about 200 feet from the place he had found him. Archie was 15 miles from his cottage.

The hotel was empty. Archie was the only guest. The owner was very happy to see Archie and very proud of his dog.

"Sit down here by the fireplace," the owner said to Archie. "Are you hungry?"

Archie suddenly felt very, very hungry. He hadn't eaten all day. "Yes, I am. I am as hungry as a ..." He was going to say that he was as hungry as a bear, but he stopped and smiled. "As a St. Bernard," he said.

"Nobody is as hungry as a St. Bernard," the owner said. "I bet $1,000 you won't be able to keep up with my St. Bernard. Beethoven, come here."

The St. Bernard came over.

"OK," Archie said. The race was on.

Archie and Beethoven had already eaten all the meals on the menu including desserts, when Archie understood he was going to lose. Beethoven ate everything! Then Archie got an idea.

"Bring us each a piece of bread," he said to the owner.

Archie ate his bread, but Beethoven didn't touch it. He had had enough and didn't care about a piece of bread. Archie won $1,000.

"I am giving the $1,000 to Beethoven," Archie said. "For saving my life."

Notes

_____

_____

I. Choose the right answer.

1. Archie and his friends went _____.
    a. on a hike
    b. on strike
    c. skiing

2. Archie was _____.
    a. lazy
    b. selfish
    c. stubborn

3. Archie's problem was that _____.
    a. he couldn't ski
    b. he got lost
    c. he was afraid of dogs

4. Archie was saved by _____.
    a. Beethoven
    b. Mozart
    c. Verdi

5. Beethoven was a _____.
    a. bear
    b. wolf
    c. dog

6. Archie _____ Beethoven.
    a. lost to
    b. won over
    c. tied with

II. **Complete the sentences with the words from the box below.**

desserts	lick	including	whispered
sniff	race	~~stubborn~~	exhausted

1. Archie always did what he wanted. He didn't listen to anybody. He was _stubborn_____.

2. Archie couldn't continue. He was very tired. He was _____.

3. Archie talked in a very low voice. He _____.

4. The bear used his nose. It started to _____ Archie.

5. The bear used his tongue. It started to _____ Archie's face.

6. Archie began to compete with Beethoven. The _____ was on.

7. Cake, pie and ice cream are _____.

8. Beethoven ate everything. He ate desserts too. He ate everything _____ desserts.

III. **Choose two words from the box on the previous page and write a short paragraph using them.**

_____
_____
_____
_____

IV. **Complete the sentences with the expressions from the box below. Use the past tense.**

won't be able to	held his breath
after all	play dead

1. Archie knew he had to pretend he was dead. He had to _____.

2. Archie didn't breathe. He _____.

3. In the end Archie was lucky. He was lucky _____.

4. The owner said, "You can't keep up with Beethoven. You _____."

V. **Choose two expressions from the box above and write a short paragraph using these expressions.**

_____
_____
_____
_____
_____

VI. Answer the questions in full sentences.

1. What was Archie doing in the mountains?
2. Who had he gone hiking with?
3. What season was it?
4. Why did his friends return to the cottage?
5. Why didn't Archie return with his friends?
6. What did Archie think he saw?
7. Who helped him and led him to a safe place?
8. What was the race against Beethoven about?
9. Why did Archie win the race?

VII. Oral Summary

Retell the story in a few sentences.

VIII. Written Summary

Write a few sentences to summarize the story.

_____
_____
_____
_____
_____
_____
_____
_____

MY FRIEND BURGLAR

Brigitte Gear was a police officer. She had been a police officer for almost ten years. She thought she had seen it all, until one day something strange happened to her.

Brigitte loved to be alone. She loved solitude. She had a cottage in the mountains. She had bought the cottage especially because there were no neighbors. The closest cottage was two miles away.

She spent a lot of her free time in the cottage. No TV, no radio, no computer. She couldn't even use her cell phone. There was no internet, no phone service. That was what she adored. Deer often came close to her cottage. There was peace and quiet.

She couldn't reach her cottage by car. She always left her car in the parking lot a mile away and walked there.

One day Brigitte was walking to her cottage when she suddenly felt something soft under her boot. She looked down, and she instantly knew that she was in trouble. She had stepped on a snake. She screamed and jumped, but it was too late. She felt as if somebody had put out a cigarette on her skin. The snake had bitten her on the leg.

Brigitte tried to think quickly. Her cottage was just two hundred feet away. She had to reach the cottage. She had a special police radio for emergency purposes there. She hoped the battery wasn't dead.

Brigitte finally reached the cottage, and she suddenly stopped. The door of the cottage was open. A man came out of the cottage and stopped too. They stared at each other for ten seconds. Then Brigitte pulled out a gun. "Put your hands up," she shouted. "And don't move!"

Suddenly Brigitte felt very sick. Then everything went black. She had fainted.

Brigitte opened her eyes. She was in the hospital. Four of her colleagues – policemen – were next to her bed. The burglar was with them.

"Thank God you woke up, Brigitte," one of the policemen said. "How are you feeling?"

"I am fine," Brigitte said.

"This man brought you to the hospital," the policeman said and pointed at the burglar. "He saved your life. He keeps saying he is your friend, but I doubt it. Is he?"

Brigitte looked at the burglar. He was a small man and looked poor. Brigitte was a big woman. "How did you manage to carry me down the mountain?" she asked him.

The man smiled showing all his white teeth. "I used to be a sherpa," he said. "It wasn't a problem for me, ma'am."

"Who is that man?" the policeman asked. "Do you know him, Brigitte?"

"Sure I do," she said. "He is my best friend."

Notes

I. **Choose the right answer.**

1. Brigitte was a _____.
    a. burglar
    b. nurse
    c. police officer

2. Brigitte loved _____.
    a. parties
    b. solitude
    c. big cities

3. Brigitte spent a lot of time _____.
    a. with her family
    b. in her cottage
    c. abroad

4. Brigitte stepped on a _____.
    a. snake
    b. hedgehog
    c. trap

5. The man at her cottage was a _____.
    a. policeman
    b. neighbor
    c. burglar

6. In the end the _____ saved her life.
    a. burglar
    b. policeman
    c. the neighbor

II. **Complete the sentences with the words from the box below.**

| fainted | instantly | ~~solitude~~ | sherpa |
| adored | reach | manage | especially |

1. Brigitte loved to be alone. She loved _solitude_.

2. She chose the cottage _____ because there were no neighbors.

3. She _____ peace and quiet.

4. It was impossible to get to the cottage by car. She couldn't _____ it by car.

5. In a fraction of a second Brigitte knew she was in trouble. She knew it _____.

6. Brigitte lost consciousness. She _____.

7. Brigitte asked the man, "How did you _____ to carry me down?"

8. It was easy for him. He used to be a _____.

III. Choose two words from the box on the previous page and write a short paragraph using them.

_____
_____
_____
_____

IV. Complete the sentences with the expressions from the box below.

emergency purposes	dead battery
put out	felt sick

1. Brigitte kept a special radio in her cottage. It was for _____.

2. Please, _____ your cigarette. You can't smoke here.

3. If a battery doesn't work anymore, we call it a _____.

4. Brigitte felt as if she was going to faint. She _____.

V. Choose two expressions from the box above and write a short paragraph using them.

_____
_____
_____
_____

VI. Answer the questions in full sentences.

1. Who was Brigitte Gear?
2. What was she like?
3. Why did she buy a cottage in the mountain?
4. Why did she walk to the cottage?
5. What happened to her one day?
6. What did she do?
7. Who was in her cottage?
8. Who saved Brigitte's life?
9. Why did Brigitte lie to her colleagues policemen?

VII. Oral Summary

Retell the story in a few sentences.

VIII. Written Summary

Write a few sentences to summarize the story.

THE COACH

My name is Stan, and I used to be a hockey player. I think hockey is the best sport that has ever been invented. It's a tough sport, and I think hockey made a man out of me. I had some ups and downs playing it, but mostly it was fun.

Anyway it is over now. I don't play hockey anymore.

You might wonder why I am telling you this. You might not even like hockey or sports. I am telling you this because I want to tell you about a special man – my coach – the man who changed my life.

One day we played the most important game of the season. It was a must win game, and everybody expected us to win.

We were sitting in the locker room. Everybody was dressed and ready for the game. We were waiting. We all knew what was coming. Suddenly the door swung open, and the coach walked in. He always started like this.

"Boys," he said. "This game is the most important thing in the world. Forget about everything now. Concentrate on the game. We are going to win."

I don't know what happened, but everything went wrong right from the beginning. We were slow and clumsy. I think the big responsibility tied our legs and hands. The other team played really well. I had never seen them play like this before.

After the first period we were down 2:0. The coach was angry. He tried everything with us. He tried to be nice. He changed the strategy a few times. Then he yelled at us and called us names. Nothing worked that night. Fifteen minutes to go, and we were losing 4:2. We were going to lose the game.

Time was running out, and the coach got really angry. He was yelling at us, he was yelling at his assistant, and he was yelling at the referees. I couldn't stand it anymore.

"Calm down Coach," I said. "It's just a game. Sometimes you win, sometimes you lose. We're doing our best. If you think it's easy, give it a try."

I didn't really mean it. The coach was 52 years old.

He looked at me for ten seconds. For me it seemed like an eternity. I expected him to explode with anger, but he didn't. "I'm not a loser," he said calmly. He turned around and suddenly he was gone.

He came back five minutes later. We couldn't believe our eyes. He was fully dressed with skates on. He started to play. It surprised our opponents and gave our team new energy. We won that night. People talked about it for years.

When I have a difficult time in my life, I always think about the coach, and I smile. "I am not a loser," I say to myself.

Notes

I. **Choose the right answer.**

1. The narrator used to be _____.
    a. a hockey coach
    b. a hockey player
    c. a hockey referee

2. The narrator said, hockey was _____.
    a. an easy sport
    b. a dirty sport
    c. a tough sport

3. That night they played _____.
    a. an ordinary game
    b. an easy game
    c. a very important game

4. Everybody expected them _____.
    a. to win
    b. to lose
    c. to tie

5. They started the game _____.
    a. very well
    b. as usual
    c. very badly

6. At the end, the coach did _____.
    a. a surprising thing
    b. a very bad thing
    c. the usual thing

II. **Complete the sentences with the words from the box below.**

responsibility	eternity	strategy	~~must win~~
calm down	concentrate	loser	stand

1. It was very important for us to win. It was a
   must win game.

2. The coach told us not to think about anything else. He told us to _____ on the game.

3. We knew the game was very important. It was a big _____ for us.

4. The coach told us exactly what to do. He told us the _____ of the game.

5. The coach's behavior was very annoying. I couldn't _____ it anymore.

6. I tried to talk to the coach about his behavior. I wanted him to _____.

7. The coach looked at me for a few seconds, but for me it seemed like an _____.

8. We could blame our coach for many things, but he was not a _____.

III. Choose two words from the box on the previous page and write a short paragraph using them.

_____
_____
_____
_____

IV. Complete the sentences with the expressions from the box below.

running out	doing our best
ups and downs	called us names

1. Sometimes I was successful. Sometimes I wasn't. I had my _____.

2. The coach's vocabulary was horrible. He _____.

3. We had very little time to do anything. The time was _____.

4. We were doing everything possible. We were _____.

V. Choose two expressions from the box above and write a short paragraph using them.

_____
_____
_____
_____

VI. Answer the questions in full sentences.

1. What sport did Stan use to play?
2. What did Stan think about hockey?
3. Why did Stan tell us the story?
4. What did the coach always say before a game?
5. Why was the game Stan told us about so important?
6. What happened at the beginning of the game?
7. How did the coach react?
8. What did Stan say to the coach?
9. What did the coach do?

VII. Oral Summary

Retell the story in a few sentences.

VIII. Written Summary

Write a few sentences to summarize the story.

THE JESTER

A long time ago in a country somewhere in Europe, there was a king. His name was Stibor. He was very rich and spent most of his time hunting and amusing himself.

One day the king and his noblemen went hunting. They rode all day through the forest looking for deer, but they couldn't find any.

The sun went down. They stopped near a high rock and got off the horses. They wanted to spend the night under the high rock. They were all very tired. The king was in a bad mood.

The noblemen tried very hard to cheer the king up and make him laugh, but nothing worked.

"Betsko, where is Betsko?" the king shouted. "Where is he hiding? I need him now."

Betsko was the king's jester.

"I am here, sire, the jester said. "I wasn't hiding. I didn't want to bother you."

"Bother me?" the king said. "You are my jester, aren't you? Make me laugh or get lost."

"All right, sire," the jester said. He was silent for a minute, and then he started to speak. "You know, you kings and noblemen, you are like spoiled children. You want your toys or you get nasty."

"Don't try my patience, jester," the king said.

"You didn't find any deer today, the jester said. "Who cares? You will find some tomorrow. The king in the neighboring country has a much bigger problem than you. No jester can help him. That's for sure."

The king was really angry now, but the jester had piqued his curiosity.

"What happened to the king?" he asked.

Betsko started to tell the king a story.

"The king's knight came to the castle with prisoners, bags of gold and other riches from his victories.

'Tell me of your battles,' the king said.

'Well, sire," the knight said. "I have been robbing and stealing on your behalf for weeks. I have burned all the villages of your enemies in the north.'

The king was horrified. 'But I have no enemies in the north,' he said.

'Well,' the knight said. 'You do now.'"

There was total silence for a few seconds. Then the king smiled and burst into wild laughter. Everybody laughed, and they couldn't stop.

"You are good, jester, the king said still laughing. "You can have one wish."

"Any wish, sire?" the jester asked.

"Yes," the king said.

"Build a castle for me on this high rock," the jester said.

The king couldn't take his word back. The castle is still standing today. They call it Betsko's castle.

Notes

_____

_____

_____

_____

_____

I. **Choose the right answer.**

1. Stibor was a _____.
    a. king
    b. stable boy
    c. jester

2. Betsko was a _____.
    a. king
    b. stable boy
    c. jester

3. The noblemen were hunting _____.
    a. deer
    b. fox
    c. bear

4. The king wanted the jester to _____.
    a. make him cry
    b. leave him alone
    c. make him laugh

5. The king laughed because _____.
    a. the jester did a headstand
    b. the jester made a funny face
    c. the jester told him a joke

6. The jester wished for _____.
    a. a bag of gold
    b. a castle
    c. a horse

II. **Complete the sentences with the words from the box below.**

| wish | riches | amusing | cheer |
| horrified | noblemen | neighboring | ~~jester~~ |

1. Betsko's job was to make the king laugh. He was his _jester_.

2. The king liked having fun. He liked _____ himself.

3. Those who went hunting with the king weren't ordinary people. They were _____.

4. The noblemen wanted to make the king laugh. They wanted to _____ him up.

5. When countries have a common border, they are _____ countries.

6. The knight brought many valuable things. He brought _____.

7. The king didn't approve of what the knight did at all. He was _____.

8. The jester could ask for one thing. He had one _____.

III. Choose two words from the box on the previous page and write a short paragraph using them.

_____
_____
_____
_____

IV. Complete the sentences with the expressions from the box below.

| take his word back | piqued his curiosity |
| get nasty | try my patience |

1. Some children _____ when you take a toy from them.

2. The king got angry. "Don't _____," he said.

3. The king wanted to know what had happened. The jester had _____.

4. The king couldn't change his mind. He couldn't _____.

V. Choose two expressions from the box above and write a short paragraph using them.

_____
_____
_____
_____

VI. Answer the questions in full sentences.

1. Where did the story happen?
2. What was King Stibor like?
3. Why was King Stibor upset during the hunt?
4. Who was Betsko?
5. What did the King say to Betsko?
6. How did Betsko make the King laugh?
7. How was the King going to reward Betsko?
8. What did Betsko wish for?
9. What is the castle called today?

VII. Oral Summary

Retell the story in a few sentences.

VIII. Written Summary

Write a few sentences to summarize the story.

_____
_____
_____
_____
_____
_____
_____
_____

A MIRACLE

One Saturday evening in February a bus was going through the mountains in Canada. The bus was full of twelve-year-old children. They were returning home from a ski trip.

Suddenly the weather changed. A strong wind started to blow heavy snow onto the road. The children didn't realize the danger. They were singing and laughing, but the driver and the teacher were very alarmed. It was getting dark, and the driver couldn't see the road ahead very well. And then it happened.

Boom! The bus had slid and crashed into a tree. The driver hurt his head badly and fell off the seat onto the floor. He wasn't moving. The teacher standing in the aisle fell onto the floor, too. She wasn't moving either. None of the children were seriously hurt because they were all sitting and wearing seatbelts, but they were in trouble. They were by themselves in the mountains, and no other buses or cars were coming.

The year was 1990. Nobody had a cell phone back then. The children tried to wake the driver and the teacher, but they couldn't. It was getting cold and some of the children started to cry.

Two hours later the situation hadn't changed.

"We are all going to die here," a boy said. Only a miracle could save us." A girl started to pray for a miracle. And a miracle happened.

A tall girl was sitting by herself. All the other children were sitting in pairs, but she was alone. Her name was Anna. She had recently arrived in Canada from another country and hadn't made any friends yet.

Anna stood up. She had been thinking about something for some time, and now she decided to act. She went to the front of the bus, and she sat in the driver's seat. She looked at the steering wheel, the gearshift and the pedals. It was not the same as her daddy's truck, but it was similar. She knew everything about trucks. Her father was a truck driver. He had let her drive his truck many times.

The key was in the ignition. Anna put her feet on the pedals and turned the key. The engine turned over and made a friendly sound.

The other children jumped up from their seats. They couldn't believe their eyes. The bus was moving, and Anna was driving it.

Anna was able to drive the bus to the nearest gas station. The gas station attendant called 911. An ambulance came and took the driver and the teacher to the hospital. The police took care of the children.

So, in the end, everybody was saved thanks to Anna. Anna became a hero. She has many friends now. When the class goes on a trip, everybody wants to sit next to her.

"I'm not surprised at what Anna did," her father said. "She's my girl."

Notes

_____
_____
_____
_____

I. **Choose the right answer.**

1. The children were _____.
    a. going on vacation in the mountains
    b. returning from a ski trip
    c. returning from school

2. Suddenly the weather _____.
    a. got nice
    b. got worse
    c. got hot

3. The bus driver _____.
    a. fell asleep while driving
    b. got lost in a snow storm
    c. crashed into a tree

4. Anna was originally from _____.
    a. the USA
    b. Mexico
    c. an unknown country

5. Anna's father was a _____.
    a. truck driver
    b. gas station attendant
    c. policeman

6. Everyone was OK thanks to _____.
    a. Anna
    b. the driver
    c. the teacher

II. **Complete the sentences with the words from the box below.**

alarmed	pedals	~~miracle~~	seatbelts
ignition	aisle	steering wheel	gearshift

1. Something amazing happened. Nobody had expected it. It was a _miracle_.

2. The driver and the teacher were worried. They were _____.

3. The teacher was standing between the seats. She was standing in the _____.

4. The children were sitting in their seats. They were wearing _____.

5. We use the _____ to change directions.

6. We use the _____ to change gears.

7. We use the _____ to brake, accelerate and change gears.

8. We put the key in the _____.

III. Choose two words from the box on the previous page and write a short paragraph using them.

_____
_____
_____
_____

IV. Complete the sentences with the expressions from the box below.

| turned over | thanks to |
| seriously hurt | back then |

1. The children were fine. Nobody was _____, but they were in trouble.

2. Children didn't use to have cell phones _____. It was not as easy as today.

3. The engine started to work. It _____.

4. Everybody on the bus was saved _____ Anna. She became a hero.

V. Choose two expressions from the box above and write a short paragraph using them.

_____
_____
_____
_____

VI. Answer the questions in full sentences.

1. Where did the story happen?
2. Who was on the bus?
3. What was the season?
4. Where were the children returning from?
5. Why were the driver and the teacher alarmed?
6. What happened?
7. What happened to the driver and to the teacher?
8. Who saved them all?
9. Why was Anna able to drive the bus?

VII. Oral Summary

Retell the story in a few sentences.

VIII. Written Summary

Write a few sentences to summarize the story.

_____
_____
_____
_____
_____
_____
_____
_____
_____

BUDDY

One Sunday morning Joe was walking to the grocery store. He usually walks there. It is not far from his house.

Joe noticed a dog sitting on the sidewalk. It was a big black dog. Joe automatically crossed the street. He didn't want to be anywhere near the dog. He was afraid of dogs. When he was a little boy, a dog bit him. He still remembered this.

Joe bought what he needed at the grocery store and began to walk home. The dog was still sitting there. Nobody was around him. Joe stopped and looked at the dog from afar. Something was wrong with the dog's leg.

Joe approached the dog slowly and looked at him more carefully. The dog was holding his leg in the air, and he was trembling. It was very cold outside. The dog was cold.

"Hey buddy," Joe said. "What's the matter with you? Where's your master?"

The dog looked at Joe with his big sad eyes.

"Don't look at me like that," Joe said. "I can't help you. Somebody else will."

Joe continued to walk home. After a few seconds he turned. The dog was following him. When he stopped, the dog stopped, too. When he began to walk, the dog followed him. The dog walked with a limp.

"Don't do that," Joe said. "I can't help you. I'm not the right person for you. I don't like dogs. I'm a cat person. I like cats."

The dog followed Joe to his house. Joe suddenly felt very sorry for the dog. He let him into the house. He gave the dog a bowl of water and a little chicken from his refrigerator. The dog ate the chicken in a few seconds and drank the whole bowl of water.

"It's just temporary," Joe said. "I hope you understand I can't keep you."

Joe drove to the vet with the dog. The vet fixed the dog's leg. Joe took good care of the dog. He tried very hard to find his owner. He put up signs and put ads in the newspaper, all in vain. He didn't know the dog's name, so he called him Buddy.

When Joe walked Buddy, and people asked him about his dog, he always said, "He's *not* my dog. I found him on the street. I'm looking for his real owner."

It had been almost a year and Joe was still looking for the owner. One day Joe was walking Buddy along the river. The river was frozen. A few boys were playing on the ice. Suddenly Joe heard a scream. "My brother! He's drowning!" The ice had broken and one of the boys had fallen into the water.

Buddy saw this. He jumped into the water and did something unbelievable. He dived three times until he found the boy and pulled him out of the water. The story was in the newspaper. Buddy became a hero.

Today when Joe walks Buddy, he proudly says to everybody. "His name is Buddy. He is *my* dog."

Notes

_____
_____
_____
_____

I. Choose the right answer.

1. Joe lived in _____.
    a. a house
    b. an apartment
    c. the street

2. Joe didn't like _____.
    a. cats
    b. dogs
    c. walking

3. Joe saw a dog and _____.
    a. called the police
    b. called a veterinarian
    c. crossed the street

4. The dog _____.
    a. attacked Joe
    b. ran away
    c. followed Joe

5. Joe _____.
    a. put the dog in an animal shelter
    b. chased the dog away
    c. kept the dog

6. The dog _____.
    a. drowned in the river
    b. saved a boy from drowning
    c. drowned a boy in the river

II. **Complete the sentences with the words from the box below.**

dived	master	buddy	signs
automatically	drowning	~~noticed~~	sidewalk

1. Joe saw a black dog. He _noticed_ him.

2. The dog was sitting on the _____.

3. Joe crossed the street without thinking. He did it _____.

4. Another word for a friend is a _____.

5. A dog's owner can be called the dog's _____.

6. A boy screamed. His brother had fallen into the water And was _____.

7. The dog went below the water. He _____.

8. Joe wanted people to read about the dog he had found. He put up _____.

III. **Choose two words from the box on the previous page and write a short paragraph using them.**

_____
_____
_____
_____

IV. **Complete the sentences with the expressions from the box below.**

walk with a limp	in vain
cat person	something was wrong

1. Joe saw that the dog's leg was hurt. He saw _____ with the dog's leg.

2. A _____ is someone who likes cats.

3. The dog couldn't walk normally because of pain in his leg. He _____.

4. Joe didn't find the dog's owner. He searched _____.

V. **Choose two expressions from the box above and write a short paragraph using them.**

_____
_____
_____
_____
_____

VI. Answer the questions in full sentences.

1. Where was Joe walking on a Sunday morning?
2. What did he see?
3. Why was he afraid of dogs?
4. What did he do?
5. What happened when Joe was walking back home?
6. Why did Joe let the dog into his house?
7. What did he do to find the dog's owner?
8. What happened one day by the river?
9. Did Joe find the owner or did he keep the dog?

VII. Oral Summary

Retell the story in a few sentences.

VIII. Written Summary

Write a few sentences to summarize the story.

_____
_____
_____
_____
_____
_____
_____
_____

THE KICKBOXER

Johannes Guttmann was only 18 years old and was already in prison. He had been sentenced to 15 years.

What crime had he committed? Had he killed somebody? No. Had he robbed a bank? No. So what had he done? What was his crime? His crime was that he had tried to cross a border illegally.

You are probably wondering which border, and why the sentence was so severe.

Well, it was 1979, and it was the border between East Germany and West Germany. Johannes had tried to get to West Germany.

In a way Johannes was lucky. He was sharing a prison cell with a former kickboxer, Rudi Steiner. Rudi was in prison for bank robbery. Johannes and Rudi had become good friends Rudi was teaching Johannes how to fight.

The years went by. Ten years later Johannes was a better kickboxer than Rudi. Rudi had taught Johannes all the kickboxing tricks he knew.

In 1989 the communist regime in East Germany finally fell and Johannes was released from prison. He was 29 with almost no education, no job, no money and a record.

Johannes was walking down the street. He saw a bank and smiled. He remembered his friend Rudi. Rudi had taught him about bank robberies, too. For a second it crossed his mind. "If I robbed a bank, I would have enough money to start a new life," he thought. "I will just look around." He walked into the bank.

"May I help you, sir," a young woman said.

Johannes looked at the woman. She was the most beautiful woman he had ever seen. "Irene," her name tag read.

"I, I am sorry. I just wanted ..." Johannes didn't have the chance to finish what he was going to say.

"This is a robbery! Everybody down on the floor!" a man shouted. "If you move, you die." There were three robbers. One was holding a gun.

Johannes was lying on the ground. "A competition," he thought with a smile.

The robbers took all the money they could and were about to leave when something unbelievable happened. First a police siren wailed in the distance. Then one of the robbers grabbed Irene and wanted to take her as a hostage.

Out of the blue, Johannes jumped to his feet and attacked the robbers. They hadn't expected this. Two of them never had the chance to react before he knocked them down. The third one was knocked down too, but he had had the time to shoot Johannes in the shoulder. Then the police arrived.

Johannes was in the hospital. He had become a hero. When Irene came to visit him with a bouquet of flowers, he told himself, "Better to be in the hospital than in prison."

Notes

I. Choose the right answer.

1. At the beginning Johannes _____.
    a. was in the hospital
    b. was at school
    c. was in prison

2. His crime was that he tried to _____.
    a. kill somebody
    b. rob a bank
    c. cross the border illegally

3. Rudi Steiner was in prison _____.
    a. for bank robbery
    b. for murder
    c. for fraud

4. Rudi Steiner used to be a _____.
    a. kickboxer
    b. boxer
    c. wrestler

5. Johannes _____ the robbers.
    a. joined
    b. praised
    c. attacked

6. Irene gave Johannes _____.
    a. money
    b. flowers
    c. a kiss

II. Complete the sentences with the words from the box below.

wailed	competition	released	robbery
chance	hostage	knocked	~~severe~~

1. The sentence was 15 years for trying to cross the border. It was really _severe_.

2. They let Johannes out of prison after 10 years. They _____ him.

3. Johannes didn't have time to finish his sentence. He didn't have the _____.

4. Three robbers entered the bank. It was a _____.

5. When two businesses do the same thing, they are in _____.

6. Everybody heard a police siren. It _____ in the distance.

7. The robbers tried to take Irene with them as a _____.

8. Johannes hit the robbers, and they fell down. He _____ them down.

III. **Choose two words from the box on the previous page and write a short paragraph using them.**

_____
_____
_____
_____

IV. **Complete the sentences with the expressions from the box below.**

crossed his mind	about to leave
a record	out of the blue

1. The robbers hadn't expected Johannes to attack. He did it _____.

2. Johannes had been in prison. He had _____.

3. Johannes thought about robbing the bank for a few seconds. It _____.

4. The robbers took the money and were ready to go. They were _____.

V. **Choose two expressions from the box above and write a short paragraph using them.**

_____
_____
_____
_____

VI. **Answer the questions in full sentences.**

1. How old was Johannes at the beginning of the story?
2. Where was he?
3. What crime had he committed?
4. How long was he supposed to be in prison?
5. Who was Rudi Steiner?
6. What did Rudi teach Johannes?
7. Why did they let Johannes out of prison sooner?
8. What was he thinking about when he saw a bank?
9. What happened in the bank?

VII. **Oral Summary**

Retell the story in a few sentences.

VIII. **Written Summary**

Write a few sentences to summarize the story.

_____
_____
_____
_____
_____
_____
_____
_____

THE RUNNER

Ted Hunter was running in the woods. It was 5:00 in the morning and still dark. Ted loved his morning runs. He loved being alone and having some time only to himself. He could think, and nobody bothered him. Every morning Ted ran in the woods for an hour. He had been doing this for years.

Suddenly Ted heard some voices. This was very unusual. He had never seen anybody in the woods at 5:00 in the morning.

Ted stopped and listened. Yes, definitely. Some men were talking. He couldn't hear what they were saying, but he could hear their voices.

Most people would have gotten scared and would have run away but not Ted. Ted used to be a soldier. He had been in combat many times. After what he had seen in combat, there was nothing he feared. He was also curious about what the men were doing.

Ted slowly walked toward the voices. He walked off the path into an area where the woods were denser. Then he saw them.

There were three men. One of them was holding a gun and a big bag with something in it. The other two were digging a hole.

"Holy cow," Ted said to himself. "What's that? It's like being in a freaking movie."

Ted hid behind a bush and watched the men. They buried the bag and covered the place with dead leaves. Then they left.

"Now what?" Ted said to himself.

He needed a shovel to dig the bag out, and the sun was already rising. He decided to do it tomorrow at dawn.

The next morning Ted was back at the place where the men had buried the bag. He was smiling. It was very exciting. He started to dig. Every ten seconds he stopped digging and listened to see if he was alone. It took him thirty minutes to dig up the bag. Nobody had bothered him. He opened the bag. The bag was full of cash. He could see there was a lot of money.

"Put the bag on the ground and step back," said a voice behind him.

Ted turned around. The men were back. He hadn't expected that. They had just buried the bag and now they were back? Very strange indeed.

Ted noticed that they were carrying two more bags. Bad luck!

"Have you forgotten something, boys?" Ted said. He was trying to distract them.

"I said step back!" the man shouted. "I have a gun." He drew a pistol from behind his back and pointed it at Ted.

Ted smiled. "You call that a gun?" he asked. "This is a gun." Suddenly Ted was holding a machine gun with thirty bullets in the magazine. "Drop the gun and lie down," he said. The men obeyed.

Ted pulled out a cell phone and dialed a number. "Sometimes I wish I weren't a cop," he said loudly and laughed.

Notes

I. Choose the right answer.

1. Ted loved _____ in the woods.
    a. running
    b. hiking
    c. walking

2. Ted heard some _____ in the woods.
    a. animals
    b. voices
    c. shots

3. When Ted heard the voices, _____.
    a. he ran away
    b. he called a ranger
    c. he walked towards the voices

4. The men he saw were _____.
    a. fighting
    b. digging
    c. singing

5. The men buried a bag full of _____.
    a. garbage
    b. coins
    c. cash

6. Ted was a _____.
    a. police officer
    b. criminal
    c. ranger

II. **Complete the sentences with the words from the box below.**

~~combat~~	magazine	denser	distract
obeyed	bullets	buried	dawn

1. Ted used to be a soldier, and he fought in a real war. He was in _combat_.

2. It was easy to hide in the area farther from the path. The woods were _____ there.

3. The men dug a hole and put the bag in it. They _____ the bag.

4. The sun had just started to rise. It was _____.

5. Ted started to talk to the men. He tried to _____ them.

6. Ted's gun had a big capacity. It held thirty _____.

7. The part of a gun where you put bullets is called a _____.

8. The men did exactly what Ted said. They _____ him.

III. **Choose two words from the box on the previous page and write a short paragraph using them.**

_____
_____
_____
_____

IV. **Complete the sentences with the expressions from the box below.**

| machine gun | dialed a number |
| dead leaves | holly cow |

1. Ted was very surprised. He said,
   " _____. "

2. Dry leaves that are on the ground in the woods are called _____.

3. Ted had a gun that shot automatically. He had a _____.

4. Ted touched some keys with numbers on his cell phone. He _____.

V. **Choose two expressions from the box above and write a short paragraph using them.**

_____
_____
_____
_____

VI. Answer the questions in full sentences.

1. What did Ted Hunter love?
2. Why did he love it?
3. What did he hear one morning while he was running?
4. Why was he surprised?
5. What did he do?
6. What did he see?
7. What was in the bag?
8. Why did the men obey Ted?
9. Who was Ted?

VII. Oral Summary

Retell the story in a few sentences.

VIII. Written Summary

Write a few sentences to summarize the story.

_____
_____
_____
_____
_____
_____
_____
_____
_____
_____

FREE AUDIO

You can download a free audio version of the book at

www.easy-reading-esl.com/freedownload6166172.html

NOTES

Printed in Great Britain
by Amazon